Nutrition

Nutrition Anyone?

Kristin Petrie

ABDO Publishing Company

visit us at
www.abdopub.com

Published by ABDO Publishing Company, 4940 Viking Drive, Edina, Minnesota 55435.
Copyright © 2004 by Abdo Consulting Group, Inc. International copyrights reserved in all countries. No part of this book may be reproduced in any form without written permission from the publisher.

Printed in the United States.

Cover Photo: Corbis
Interior Photos: Corbis pp. 1, 5, 7, 9, 11, 13, 14-15, 16, 17, 21, 23, 25, 27, 28; U.S. Department of Agriculture and U.S. Department of Health and Human Services p. 29

Editors: Kate A. Conley, Stephanie Hedlund, Kristianne E. Vieregger
Art Direction: Neil Klinepier

Library of Congress Cataloging-in-Publication Data

Petrie, Kristin, 1970-
   Nutrition anyone? / Kristin Petrie.
      p. cm. -- (Nutrition)
   Summary: Discusses what nutrition is, how what we eat affects our bodies, the importance of good nutrition, the digestive process, and more.
   Includes bibliographical references and index.
   ISBN 1-59197-404-6
   1. Nutrition--Juvenile literature. [1. Nutrition.] I. Title.

QP141.P456 2003
613.2--dc21
                                                        2002043620

Contents

Nutrition

Nutrition is a type of science. It is the study of food and what our bodies do with it. Why do we need to understand nutrition? Let us count the ways!

Actually, it would take hours and hours to count the many ways that eating affects us. We could never finish because new discoveries about nutrition are made every day.

How you eat affects everything about you. Food even provides the energy for you to read this book! Continue reading to learn how nutrition affects us in visible and invisible ways.

Studying Nutrition

Who studies nutrition? Nutritionists do! These scientists study how eating the right nutrients affects our bodies. Nutritionists work at schools, hospitals, and even in laboratories.

Opposite page: Your body's energy demands are very high. You need extra calories because you are still building bones and muscle.

You Are What You Eat

"You are what you eat." You've heard this phrase before. But, did you really believe it? After all, you certainly don't look like a peanut butter sandwich or a carrot! Nevertheless, this statement is true.

Every one of us is really a mass of **molecules**. They are well organized, and they are constantly moving and changing. These molecules come from **nutrients** in the foods we have eaten.

Molecules are very small, but when they come together, they form all of your body parts. This happens because your body knows how to use the nutrients from food.

Consider what happens after eating a ham and cheese sandwich. Some of the proteins in the ham will become muscles, which help you sprint to the bus. At the same time, some of the carbohydrates in the bread feed your brain, which helps you recall the answers to

Your Body Is a Builder

How do nutrients turn into you? Think of a bunch of Legos. When Legos are scattered on the floor, they don't seem very important. However, when you, the builder, make a plan and put the pieces together, they form all kinds of shapes and usable structures.

test questions. And, the broken-down fats from the cheese help your skin heal the scrape on your knee. So, you really are what you eat!

Just like when you build with Legos, your body uses a plan (**genetic** information) to put its bricks (**molecules**) together to form a structure (skeleton, muscles, and **organs**). All of your "pieces" are made from the broken-down, tiny particles that once made up **nutrients** in the foods you have eaten.

You are made up of millions of molecules that are constantly changing as you grow.

Pizza, Anyone?

Are you having pizza for lunch? Great! Let's look at a few of your body's functions and how they use the **nutrients** from the pizza.

First, you use your eyes to look at the pizza. The different parts of your eyes are made of **tissue**. It, in turn, is made of protein provided by the pizza's meat and cheese. Even your ability to see is affected by your intake of nutrients such as **vitamin** A, which can be found in the pizza's tomato sauce.

Next, you open your mouth to take a bite. Foods with carbohydrates, such as the pizza crust, provide the energy to move all your body parts, including your mouth. And, chewing is easier when you have strong teeth. They are made from calcium and other **minerals** gained from the foods you have eaten.

Now the pizza moves to your stomach and intestines. These **organs** are the first step in distributing food particles to their next homes. Minerals in the pizza, such as sodium and potassium, send signals to these organs. The signals tell the organs to mix up, break down, and absorb food nutrients.

After being absorbed into the blood, **nutrients** gained from your pizza need help traveling to their new homes. This help is provided by fat. While fat is mostly thought of as a bad thing in today's society, it is actually needed in moderate amounts to help nutrients travel. The cheese and meats from your pizza provide fat.

Your cells use energy and nutrients to form new cells that make up your various body parts. You get energy and nutrients from the pizza crust, cheese, tomatoes, meat, and everything else you like on your pizza. So with the help of nutrients you have already eaten, your pizza has turned into you!

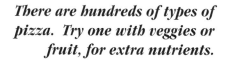

There are hundreds of types of pizza. Try one with veggies or fruit, for extra nutrients.

From Nutrients to You

Your body parts are constantly being replaced with the help of the food you eat. Different **nutrients** provide the raw materials and energy to let these processes take place. Let's look at a few body parts that are replaced.

Look at the skin on your hand. It looks the same as it did yesterday, last week, and even when you were born, right? The truth, however, is that your skin completely replaces itself about every seven years.

Now push on your skin to the softness beneath it. That softness is fat. Fat protects your **organs** and keeps you warm. But, it is not the same fat that was there just one year ago! That's because it, too, replaces itself regularly.

Your blood is constantly being replaced, too! The next time you cut your finger or scrape your knee, be amazed that the oldest red blood cell is less than 120 days old. Even more amazing, the entire surface of your **digestive** tract is replaced with new cells every three days!

Each of these repair and replace processes can only occur when you eat. Food, and everything that happens to it after you eat, has a huge impact on keeping you, YOU.

Vegetables fresh from the farm have the most nutrients. After they are picked, vegetables begin to lose their vitamin value.

Keep Going

Another more obvious need we all have is to replace the energy we use. Running to the bus, thinking for a test, playing at recess, or practicing your band instrument all require energy.

Hunger is the brain's way of telling your body to stop and refuel. When you don't refuel, your body has ways to use your **nutrient** storage. This means that if you miss a meal, your body can keep working.

If your body has stored enough nutrients, it will have the energy and raw materials it needs. But if there is a shortage of nutrients, your body will not function as well. For example, taking a test in the morning may be more difficult if you skipped breakfast. That's because your brain functions best when it doesn't have to dig deep into your storage areas for fuel.

Food as Fuel

You burn energy fastest while doing strenuous activities, such as running. Think of the last time you did a lot of running on the playground. You may have felt hungry a couple hours later. So, you probably ate a snack. It renewed your energy and allowed you to play again.

Opposite page: Keeping your brain active requires a lot of energy.

How does it feel to be low on **nutrients**? You may feel tired or even a bit crabby. Or, you might be too cold or too hot because your body needs energy to regulate its temperature. You may find yourself sick more often because nutrients help your body fight off germs and heal itself. So, making good decisions, exercising, or taking tests are all easier if you are well nourished.

Nutrients in Food

Foods we eat are made of many **molecules**. These molecules are joined together to form **nutrients**. If you could take apart a food, such as a slice of bread, you would see that the solid part of it is mostly carbohydrate, with some protein and a bit of fat. If you take away those larger pieces, you are left with tiny amounts of **vitamins** and **minerals**.

In fact, very few foods contain a single nutrient. The amount of nutrients found in these foods is what makes them different from each other. So, even though bread is usually called a carbohydrate, it is really a carbohydrate-rich food. Similarly, beef, which is mostly protein, is a protein-rich food.

What Are You Made Of?

It's hard to believe, but our bodies are made of almost the exact same stuff! If we could take apart the human body, we would find that more than half of it is water. The other half is divided between carbohydrates, protein, fat, bone minerals, and other substances.

Making different foods with friends is a great way to have fun and stay healthy.

Types of Nutrients

There are six types of **nutrients**. They are carbohydrates, fat, protein, water, **vitamins**, and **minerals**. Large nutrients are called macronutrients. Smaller nutrients are called micronutrients.

Carbohydrates, protein, water, and fat are macronutrients. Carbohydrates are your body's main source of energy. Fat also provides energy and insulates your body. Protein is needed for growing and repairing your cells. Water is necessary for all body functions, such as transporting nutrients and regulating body temperature.

We get lots of our vitamins and minerals from fresh vegetables.

Vitamins and **minerals** are micronutrients. They have different jobs than macronutrients. Vitamins and minerals help the other **nutrients** break down, absorb into your body, and nourish you.

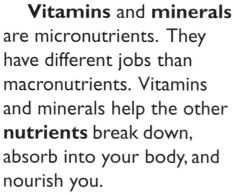

Eating a balanced meal is important. Every food you eat has different nutrients that your body needs.

The Energy Nutrients

We get energy from three of the four macronutrients. Protein, carbohydrates, and fat are macronutrients that provide energy. Energy from macronutrients helps your body do work, helps rebuild your body parts, or leaves your body as heat.

Calories Count		
1 gram of carbs	=	4 calories
1 gram of protein	=	4 calories
1 gram of fat	=	9 calories

The amount of energy that comes from food is measured in a term that is probably familiar to you. It is called a calorie. Calories are often thought of as an actual part of food. However, we cannot see or chew them. The amount of calories in a certain food depends on how much carbohydrate, protein, or fat it contains.

Think for a moment of a lima bean. If that lima bean weighed one gram and were made of pure carbohydrate, it would give four calories of energy. Similarly, that lima bean would give four calories if it were pure protein. A lima bean of pure fat, however, would give nine calories. So, knowing the number of calories provided by different foods is important!

It is also important to know that the body uses the three energy **nutrients** equally. Any unused calories are stored as fat. Therefore, eating too many calories from carbohydrates, protein, or fat will cause you to gain body fat. But, if you eat about as many calories as you use, all the energy provided by your food will be used.

How to Read a Nutrition Label

The number of calories listed for a food shows how much energy it will give. ■

A gram is a method of weighing something. This product has 6 grams of fat and 29 grams of carbohydrates. ■

The percentage shows how much of your daily requirement those grams fill. In total, this snack has 29 grams of carbohydrates. This is equal to 10 percent of the amount of carbohydrates you should eat in a day. ■

Vitamins and minerals are often listed below the energy nutrients. ■

Below all of the nutrients, a daily values chart is given. It shows the amount of some energy nutrients that a person should have based on the amount of calories he or she eats every day. The ingredients of the product are also included. ■

Nutrition Facts

Serving Size 1 pouch (42g)
Servings Per Container 6

Amount Per Serving	Oats N' Honey or Cinnamon		Peanut Butter	
Calories	180		180	
Calories from Fat	50		50	
		%DV*		%DV*
Total Fat	6g	**9%**	6g	**9%**
Saturated Fat	0.5g	**3%**	1g	**4%**
Cholesterol	0mg	**0%**	0mg	**0%**
Sodium	160mg	**7%**	170mg	**7%**
Total Carbohydrate	29g	**10%**	29g	**10%**
Dietary Fiber	2g	**8%**	2g	**8%**
Sugars	11g		11g	
Protein	4g		5g	
Iron		6%		6%

Not a significant source of vitamin A, vitamin C and calcium.

*Percent Daily Values (DV) are based on a 2,000 calorie diet. Your daily values may be higher or lower depending on your calorie needs:

	Calories:	2,000	2,500
Total Fat	Less than	65g	80g
Sat Fat	Less than	20g	25g
Cholesterol	Less than	300mg	300mg
Sodium	Less than	2,400mg	2,400mg
Total Carbohydrate		300g	375g
Dietary Fiber		25g	30g

Calories per gram: Fat 9 • Carbohydrate 4 • Protein 4

PEANUT BUTTER INGREDIENTS: WHOLE GRAIN ROLLED OATS, SUGAR, CANOLA OIL, PEANUT BUTTER (PEANUTS, PEANUT FLOUR, CORN SYRUP SOLIDS, SUGAR, SALT), CRISP RICE (RICE FLOUR, SUGAR, MALT, SALT), HONEY, SOY PROTEIN, BROWN SUGAR SYRUP, SALT, DRIED CORN SYRUP, NATURAL FLAVOR, SOY LECITHIN, BAKING SODA, ALMOND FLOUR
CONTAINS PEANUT, SOY AND ALMOND INGREDIENTS

Helper Nutrients

Your body can't function without the help of **vitamins** and **minerals**. Many of these micronutrients help the body to **digest**, absorb, and use the **nutrients** we get from food. Others act as **antioxidants**.

Every day, research uncovers new ways in which vitamins and minerals protect us from diseases such as **cancer** and heart disease. Antioxidant vitamins and minerals may even keep you looking youthful. Staying "like a kid" may not sound nice to you now, but when you are older, you will appreciate that you ate your fruits and vegetables!

Minerals are smaller than vitamins. However, they are just as important. Some minerals help your body with digestion and making energy. Others actually make up body parts, such as teeth and bones. Take calcium, for example. There is more calcium in your body than any other mineral. Can you guess where it is found? In your bones, of course!

Without enough calcium from your food, your body steals it from your bones to make sure all its other functions can take place. Not getting enough calcium from the food you eat leaves your bones weak and more likely to break. It also makes your bones less able to heal if you have been injured. The most important time to build strong, healthy bones is right now!

Eating foods packed with vitamins and minerals helps your body stay healthy.

Digestion & Metabolism

When you want to build something new with Legos that you have already made into a building, you break down that building and start over, right? The process works the same way in your body. In the body, breaking down food to get to the smaller, more usable **nutrients** is called **digestion**.

Digestion starts even before you put food in your mouth. Just the sight of food causes **enzymes** from the salivary glands in your mouth to be released. These enzymes start to break down some foods as soon as you eat them.

Metabolism starts after foods have been broken down and absorbed. Metabolism is the process where your body uses the nutrient pieces to produce energy and rebuild. It stores the extras. This process is like putting together a new Lego building. Most of the pieces are used, but some are set aside for later.

A high metabolism means your body burns energy quickly. Most healthy children have high metabolisms.

How Healthy Are You?

Eating healthy food will ensure your body has what it needs for energy and rebuilding. Since you really are what you eat, you can see that your health depends on how well you eat. When you frequently eat foods that have few **nutrients**, your body will suffer.

We all eat differently. Most of us eat foods with lots of nutrients, as well as those with few nutrients. Luckily, our bodies can manage with an intake that's less than perfect. Our bodies just need us to eat well most of the time.

If what you eat does not match your body's needs for too long, your body will take the nutrients from your bones, muscles, and other storage areas. However, the body has to work much harder to get energy and materials this way and may make you feel tired or sick. This is called malnutrition.

Happy Thoughts

Nutrition is also important to your mental well-being. Why? Eating is fun! Eating is a great time to be together with family and friends. Eating restores your physical energy and nutrients as well as your emotional needs.

Malnutrition can affect us at any age. That is why it is never too early or too late to eat a healthy diet.

Malnutrition

Overnutrition and undernutrition are both forms of malnutrition. Both conditions result when intake does not match the body's needs. The amount of energy **nutrients** that your body needs is mostly decided by how active you are. The **genetic** information inherited from your parents is an important factor as well.

Malnutrition cannot always be seen. Eating the same amount of calories as you burn can keep the body from being too thin or too heavy. Eating healthy food, however, ensures that your body has the right nutrients to stay healthy. If your body gets too many or too few nutrients over a long time period, the signs will show in how you look.

Eating too few energy nutrients leaves a person looking skinny. This is called undernutrition. Overnutrition occurs when a person eats too many energy nutrients. This leaves a person overweight. Energy is invisible and does not weigh anything, until it is left unused and turned into body fat!

Nutritionists help people learn about nutrition and how eating affects their bodies.

Your Smart Body

Understanding nutrition will help you to admire and appreciate the miracle of your body. It is not an empty container! It is far smarter and more complex than the world's greatest computer. Have fun knowing that chewing is just the start of an incredible process. This process results in energy, amazing changes in your body, and the ability to think and move.

The body is very smart and works hard to keep you going. Understanding this will also help you to wade through the nutrition misinformation that you may encounter. Most

How healthy are you?

How Well Do You Eat?

Write down what you eat for three days. Then, study your eating habits. Are you giving your body enough proper nutrition?

false information about nutrition is based on the idea that the body listens to us. Actually, just the opposite is true. The body works to keep you in balance. Sometimes that means throwing away the garbage, storing the extras, or pulling from your storage when necessary. Following the recommended servings on the **Food Guide Pyramid** can keep your body in balance.

The Food Guide Pyramid

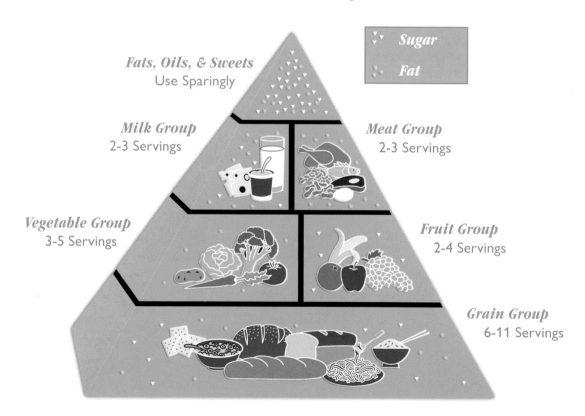

Fats, Oils, & Sweets
Use Sparingly

Sugar
Fat

Milk Group
2-3 Servings

Meat Group
2-3 Servings

Vegetable Group
3-5 Servings

Fruit Group
2-4 Servings

Grain Group
6-11 Servings

Glossary

antioxidant - a substance that protects your cells from damage.

cancer - any of a group of often deadly diseases characterized by an abnormal growth of cells that destroys healthy tissues and organs.

digest - to break down food into substances small enough for the body to absorb.

enzyme - a complex protein produced in the living cells of all plants and animals. It is used in many of the body's functions, from digestion to clotting.

Food Guide Pyramid - a chart used to describe dietary guidelines for Americans.

genetic - of or relating to the branch of biology that deals with the principles of heredity.

metabolism - the process by which all living things turn food into energy.

mineral - a tiny, inorganic molecule that does not give energy but is needed in small amounts by the body.

molecule - the smallest piece of a substance that is still the same substance. A molecule breaks down into one or more atoms.

nutrient - a substance found in food and used in the body to promote growth, maintenance, and repair.

organ - a part of an animal or plant that is composed of several kinds of tissues and that performs a specific function. The heart, liver, gallbladder, and intestines are organs in an animal.

tissue - a group or cluster of similar cells that work together, such as a muscle.

vitamin - a tiny, organic molecule that does not give energy but is needed in small amounts by the body.

Saying It

antioxidant - an-tee-AHK-suh-duhnt
calcium - KAL-see-uhm
carbohydrate - kahr-boh-HI-drayt
enzyme - EN-zIme

macronutrient - MA-kroh-NOO-tree-uhnt
malnutrition - mal-noo-TRIH-shuhn
metabolism - muh-TA-buh-lih-zuhm
micronutrient - MI-kroh-NOO-tree-uhnt

Web Sites

To learn more about nutrition, visit ABDO Publishing Company on the World Wide Web at **www.abdopub.com**. Web sites about nutrition are featured on our Book Links page. These links are routinely monitored and updated to provide the most current information available.

Index